BABY SHOWER

_____

_____

_____

_____

_____

Name	Gift

Name	Gift

Name	Gift

Name	Gift

Name	Gift

Name	Gift

Name	Gift

Name	Gift

www.ingramcontent.com/pod-product-compliance
Lightning Source LLC
Chambersburg PA
CBHW060504240426
43661CB00007B/905